GW01397898

# COOKING WITH FLAVOR

JIM STEPHENS

# COOKING WITH FLAVOR

## DELICIOUS RECIPES FOR EVERY PALATE

QuantumQuill Press

# CONTENTS

# CONTENTS

Copyright © 2024 by Jim Stephens

All rights reserved. No part of this book may be reproduced in any manner what-
soever without written permission except in the case of brief quotations em-
bodied in critical articles and reviews.

First Printing, 2024

# CHAPTER 1: INTRODUCTION TO COOKING WITH FLAVOR

In the vast realm of culinary arts, flavor reigns supreme. It's the essence that tantalizes our taste buds, evokes memories, and elevates a meal from mere sustenance to a memorable experience. In this chapter, we embark on a journey to explore the fundamental aspects of cooking with flavor, delving into its significance, understanding various flavor profiles, and discovering techniques to enhance flavor in your dishes.

Understanding the Importance of Flavor in Cooking:

Flavor is not merely about taste; it encompasses a multi-sensory experience that engages our senses of taste, smell, and even sight. It is what distinguishes one dish from another, one chef's signature creation from another's. The importance of flavor in cooking cannot be overstated, as it is the primary factor that determines the success and enjoyment of a dish.

- Taste: The Foundation of Flavor - Taste, often referred to as the basic tastes, includes sweet, sour, salty, bitter, and umami. Each taste contributes to the overall flavor profile of a dish, and mastering the balance between them is essential for creating harmonious flavors.
- Aromas: The Scent of Flavor - A significant component of flavor is aroma, which arises from volatile compounds released during cooking. Aroma plays a crucial role in our perception of flavor, influencing our expectations and enhancing our dining experience.
- Texture: The Feel of Flavor - Texture adds another dimension to flavor, providing contrast and interest to a dish. From crispiness to creaminess, texture affects how we perceive and enjoy different foods.

Exploring Different Flavor Profiles:

Flavor profiles refer to the characteristic combination of tastes, aromas, and textures that define a particular dish or cuisine. Each cuisine has its distinct flavor profile, influenced by factors such as geography, culture, and culinary traditions.

- Mediterranean: The Flavors of the Sun - Mediterranean cuisine is renowned for its emphasis on fresh, vibrant ingredients such as olive oil, tomatoes, garlic, and herbs like basil and oregano. It's a celebration of simplicity and purity, where flavors shine through in every bite.
- Asian: A Symphony of Sweet, Sour, Salty, and Spicy - Asian cuisine encompasses a diverse range of flavors, from the umami-rich dishes of Japan to the fiery spices of Thailand and the complex flavors of Indian curries.

It's a fusion of sweet, sour, salty, and spicy elements that create a harmonious balance on the palate.

· Latin American: The Vibrant Flavors of the Tropics - Latin American cuisine is a melting pot of flavors, influenced by indigenous ingredients, European culinary traditions, and African spices. From tangy ceviche to savory empanadas and fiery salsas, it's a celebration of bold, vibrant flavors.

How to Enhance Flavor in Your Dishes:

While some ingredients naturally possess robust flavors, others may require coaxing to reach their full potential. Fortunately, there are various techniques and ingredients you can employ to enhance the flavor of your dishes and elevate them to new heights.

· Layering Flavors: Building Complexity - Layering flavors involves adding ingredients at different stages of cooking to develop depth and complexity. Whether it's caramelizing onions to enhance their sweetness or deglazing a pan with wine to add acidity, each step contributes to the overall flavor profile of the dish.

· Balancing Tastes: Achieving Harmony - Achieving balance is key to creating well-rounded flavors in your dishes. Experiment with the interplay of sweet, sour, salty, bitter, and umami tastes to find the perfect equilibrium that pleases your palate.

· Enhancing Aromas: Perfuming Your Dishes - Aromatics such as garlic, onions, herbs, and spices are the building blocks of flavor in many cuisines. By sautéing aromatics at the beginning of cooking or adding fresh herbs as a finishing touch, you can infuse your dishes with enticing aromas that enhance their overall appeal.

In the journey of cooking with flavor, understanding its importance, exploring different flavor profiles, and mastering techniques to enhance flavor are essential steps. By embracing the art and science of flavor, you'll embark on a culinary adventure filled with creativity, satisfaction, and delicious discoveries. So, let's dive in and savor every moment of this flavorful journey.

# CHAPTER 2: THE BASICS OF FLAVOR BUILDING

In the culinary world, mastering the art of flavor building is akin to wielding a painter's brush on a canvas, creating intricate and harmonious compositions that delight the senses. In this chapter, we delve into the foundational elements of flavor building, from the five basic tastes to the elusive fifth taste of umami, and explore the delicate balance between sweet, sour, salty, bitter, and umami flavors.

Understanding the Five Basic Tastes:

Taste is the cornerstone of flavor, encompassing five primary sensations that our taste buds can detect: sweet, sour, salty, bitter, and umami.

1. Sweet: Sweetness is perhaps the most universally beloved taste, associated with sugar and sugary substances. It can evoke feelings of pleasure and satisfaction, making

it a crucial component in desserts, baked goods, and many savory dishes.

2. Sour: Sourness is characterized by acidity and tartness, often found in citrus fruits, vinegar, and fermented foods like yogurt and sauerkraut. Sour flavors add brightness and balance to dishes, cutting through richness and enhancing other taste sensations.

3. Salty: Saltiness is one of the most fundamental tastes, essential for enhancing flavor and preserving foods. Salt can heighten the perception of other tastes, making ingredients more vibrant and savory. However, moderation is key, as excessive saltiness can overpower other flavors.

4. Bitter: Bitterness is often associated with substances like coffee, dark chocolate, and certain vegetables like kale and arugula. While bitterness can be off-putting in excess, it adds depth and complexity to dishes when balanced with other tastes.

5. Umami: Umami, often described as savory or meaty, is the fifth basic taste that was identified relatively recently compared to the others. It is found in foods rich in glutamate, such as tomatoes, mushrooms, soy sauce, and aged cheeses. Umami adds a depth of flavor and richness to dishes, enhancing their overall complexity.

Exploring Umami: The Fifth Taste:

Umami, a Japanese word that translates to "pleasant savory taste," was officially recognized as the fifth basic taste in the early 20th century by Japanese chemist Kikunae Ikeda. Umami is characterized by a savory, mouthwatering sensation that is distinct from the other tastes.

- Umami-Rich Ingredients: Umami is abundant in certain foods that are naturally rich in glutamate, an amino acid responsible for its characteristic taste. Ingredients such as tomatoes, mushrooms, soy sauce, Parmesan cheese, and seaweed are prized for their umami flavor.
- Enhancing Umami: While umami is inherent in many foods, there are techniques to enhance its presence in dishes. Fermentation, aging, and slow cooking can all intensify umami flavors, as can combining umami-rich ingredients to create synergistic effects.
- Umami in Culinary Traditions: Umami has long been celebrated in various culinary traditions around the world, from Italian cuisine's use of Parmesan cheese and tomatoes to Japanese cuisine's reliance on dashi broth and fermented soy products like miso and soy sauce.

Balancing Sweet, Sour, Salty, Bitter, and Umami:

Achieving balance between the five basic tastes is key to creating well-rounded and satisfying flavor profiles in your dishes. By carefully calibrating the ratios of sweet, sour, salty, bitter, and umami elements, you can create dishes that are complex, harmonious, and deeply satisfying.

- The Yin and Yang of Flavor: In many culinary traditions, balance is often conceptualized as a harmony between opposing forces, such as sweet and sour or salty and bitter. Balancing these contrasting tastes creates a dynamic interplay of flavors that excites the palate.
- Experimenting with Flavor Combinations: Don't be afraid to experiment with different flavor combinations to find what works best for your palate. Whether it's pairing

sweet fruits with salty cheeses, sour citrus with umami-rich seafood, or bitter greens with rich meats, the possibilities are endless.

· Mindful Seasoning: Seasoning is a crucial aspect of flavor balancing, as it allows you to adjust the taste of your dishes to achieve the desired flavor profile. Taste and season your dishes as you cook, making adjustments as needed to ensure perfect balance.

In the art of flavor building, understanding the five basic tastes, embracing the nuances of umami, and achieving harmony between sweet, sour, salty, bitter, and umami flavors are essential skills. By mastering these fundamentals, you'll unlock a world of culinary creativity and create dishes that delight the senses and nourish the soul. So, let your taste buds be your guide as you embark on this flavorful journey of discovery.

# CHAPTER 3: HERBS AND SPICES: THE KEY TO FLAVORFUL DISHES

Herbs and spices are the alchemists of the kitchen, transforming ordinary ingredients into extraordinary culinary creations. In this chapter, we delve into the role of herbs and spices in flavor enhancement, identify essential herbs and spices for every kitchen, and explore the art of pairing them to unlock maximum flavor potential.

Understanding the Role of Herbs and Spices:

Herbs and spices are aromatic plant-based ingredients used to season and flavor food. They add depth, complexity, and character to dishes, elevating them from mundane to memorable.

- Herbs: Herbs are the leaves of plants used for flavoring and garnishing. They can be used fresh or dried and are prized for their aromatic qualities and delicate flavors. Common culinary herbs include basil, thyme, rosemary, parsley, cilantro, and mint.
- Spices: Spices are derived from the seeds, bark, roots, or fruits of plants and are known for their intense flavors and aromas. Spices can be used whole, ground, or as pastes and add warmth, depth, and complexity to dishes. Common spices include cinnamon, cumin, ginger, turmeric, paprika, and chili powder.
- Versatility: Herbs and spices can be used in a variety of culinary applications, from seasoning meats and vegetables to flavoring soups, stews, sauces, and marinades. They can also be used to create aromatic rubs, blends, and infusions that add depth and complexity to dishes.

Essential Herbs and Spices for Every Kitchen:

While the world of herbs and spices is vast and diverse, there are several essential herbs and spices that every kitchen should have on hand. These versatile ingredients form the foundation of countless recipes and are indispensable for adding flavor to a wide range of dishes.

- Herbs: Basil, parsley, thyme, rosemary, cilantro, and mint are staples in many cuisines and can be used to flavor everything from pasta sauces to salads to cocktails.
- Spices: Cumin, cinnamon, paprika, ginger, turmeric, and chili powder are essential spices that add warmth, depth, and complexity to dishes from around the world.

- Blends: In addition to individual herbs and spices, pre-made blends such as Italian seasoning, curry powder, and Cajun seasoning can be convenient shortcuts for adding flavor to dishes.

Pairing Herbs and Spices for Maximum Flavor:

Pairing herbs and spices is an art form that requires an understanding of flavor profiles, aromas, and culinary traditions. By combining complementary ingredients, you can create harmonious flavor combinations that elevate your dishes to new heights.

- Complementary Pairings: Some herbs and spices naturally complement each other, creating balanced and harmonious flavor profiles. For example, basil and tomatoes, cilantro and lime, and cinnamon and nutmeg are classic pairings that enhance each other's flavors.
- Contrasting Pairings: On the other hand, contrasting pairings can create dynamic flavor combinations that excite the palate. Pairing spicy chili powder with cooling mint or tart lemon with earthy cumin can create a complex interplay of flavors that keeps diners coming back for more.
- Experimentation: Don't be afraid to experiment with different herb and spice combinations to discover your own unique flavor combinations. Keep a well-stocked spice rack and pantry, and don't hesitate to try new ingredients and flavor pairings in your cooking.

In the art of cooking, herbs and spices are the secret ingredients that elevate dishes from ordinary to extraordinary. By understanding their role, stocking your kitchen with essential herbs and spices, and experimenting with pairings, you'll unlock a world of flavor possibilities and delight your taste buds with every bite. So, let your creativity be your guide as you embark on a flavorful journey of culinary exploration.

# CHAPTER 4: FLAVORFUL STARTERS AND APPETIZERS

The journey of a meal begins with the tantalizing flavors of starters and appetizers. In this chapter, we explore mouthwatering appetizers to kickstart your meal, flavorful dips, salsas, and sauces that tantalize the taste buds, and creative ways to serve appetizers with maximum flavor.

Mouthwatering Appetizers to Kickstart Your Meal:

Appetizers are the opening act of any culinary experience, setting the stage for the flavors to come. From light and refreshing salads to indulgent finger foods, there's an appetizer to suit every palate and occasion.

- Bruschetta with Tomato and Basil: Crispy slices of toasted baguette topped with ripe tomatoes, fresh basil, garlic, and a drizzle of olive oil. This classic Italian appetizer is bursting with flavor and perfect for showcasing the season's freshest ingredients.

· Stuffed Mushrooms with Garlic and Parmesan: Earthy mushrooms stuffed with a savory mixture of garlic, Parmesan cheese, breadcrumbs, and herbs. These bite-sized delights are packed with umami-rich flavor and make a deliciously satisfying appetizer or hors d'oeuvre.

· Shrimp Cocktail with Homemade Cocktail Sauce: Succulent shrimp served with a zesty homemade cocktail sauce made from ketchup, horseradish, Worcestershire sauce, lemon juice, and hot sauce. This timeless classic is simple yet elegant, making it the perfect starter for any occasion.

Flavorful Dips, Salsas, and Sauces:

Dips, salsas, and sauces are versatile condiments that add depth and flavor to a wide range of appetizers. Whether served alongside chips and crudites or used as a topping for grilled meats and seafood, these flavorful accompaniments are sure to please.

· Guacamole with Tortilla Chips: Creamy avocado mashed with lime juice, cilantro, onion, and tomato, seasoned with salt and pepper. This classic Mexican dip is bursting with fresh flavor and pairs perfectly with crispy tortilla chips for a satisfying snack or appetizer.

· Hummus with Pita Bread: Smooth and creamy chickpea dip flavored with tahini, garlic, lemon juice, and olive oil, served with warm pita bread for dipping. This Middle Eastern favorite is packed with protein and fiber, making it a healthy and delicious choice for any occasion.

- Chimichurri Sauce with Grilled Steak: A vibrant green sauce made from parsley, garlic, olive oil, vinegar, and red pepper flakes, traditionally served with grilled steak or other grilled meats. This tangy and herbaceous sauce adds a burst of flavor to grilled dishes and is sure to impress your guests.

Creative Ways to Serve Appetizers with Maximum Flavor:

Presentation is key when it comes to serving appetizers, as it can elevate the dining experience and enhance the enjoyment of the flavors. Get creative with your presentation to wow your guests and make your appetizers stand out.

- Skewered Appetizers: Skewers are a fun and interactive way to serve appetizers, allowing guests to enjoy bite-sized portions of their favorite flavors. Try skewering grilled vegetables, marinated meats, or fresh fruit for a colorful and flavorful appetizer display.
- Miniature Bites: Miniature versions of classic appetizers are not only adorable but also perfect for parties and gatherings where guests may be mingling and socializing. Serve mini sliders, stuffed mushrooms, or bite-sized bruschetta for a memorable appetizer experience.
- Edible Containers: Think outside the box when it comes to serving appetizers by using edible containers like cucumber cups, wonton wrappers, or phyllo pastry shells. These creative vessels add an element of whimsy to your appetizer presentation and can be filled with a variety of delicious fillings.

In the world of appetizers, the possibilities are endless. From mouthwatering starters to flavorful dips, salsas, and sauces, there's no shortage of delicious options to kickstart your meal. Get creative with your presentation and don't be afraid to experiment with flavors to create appetizers that are sure to impress your guests and leave them craving more. So, let your culinary imagination run wild as you explore the world of flavor-packed appetizers and set the stage for an unforgettable dining experience.

# CHAPTER 5: SOUPS AND SALADS BURSTING WITH FLAVOR

Soups and salads offer a canvas for creativity in the kitchen, allowing flavors to mingle and shine. In this chapter, we'll explore hearty soups packed with flavorful ingredients, vibrant salads with creative dressings, and tips for elevating the flavor of these beloved dishes.

Hearty Soups Packed with Flavorful Ingredients:

There's something inherently comforting about a steaming bowl of soup, brimming with hearty ingredients and rich flavors. From creamy bisques to chunky stews, soups offer endless possibilities for flavor exploration.

- Chicken Noodle Soup with Homemade Broth: A classic comfort food made with tender chicken, egg noodles, carrots, celery, onions, and a homemade broth flavored with aromatic herbs and spices. This soul-soothing soup is perfect for chilly days and makes a satisfying meal any time of year.

- Butternut Squash Soup with Coconut Milk and Curry: Velvety smooth butternut squash soup infused with aromatic curry spices and creamy coconut milk. This exotic twist on a traditional favorite is bursting with flavor and perfect for warming up on cold winter nights.
- Beef and Vegetable Stew with Red Wine: A hearty stew made with tender chunks of beef, root vegetables, tomatoes, and aromatic herbs, simmered to perfection in rich red wine. This rustic and flavorful dish is the epitome of comfort food and is sure to satisfy even the heartiest appetites.

Vibrant Salads with Creative Dressings:

Salads are a celebration of freshness, color, and flavor, offering a refreshing contrast to hearty soups and other main dishes. With a creative dressing and a variety of toppings, salads can be transformed into vibrant and satisfying meals.

- Mediterranean Salad with Feta and Olives: A colorful salad featuring crisp lettuce, ripe tomatoes, cucumbers, red onions, Kalamata olives, and tangy feta cheese, tossed in a lemon-herb vinaigrette. This refreshing salad captures the flavors of the Mediterranean and is perfect for summer gatherings.
- Asian-Inspired Slaw with Sesame Ginger Dressing: A crunchy and flavorful slaw made with shredded cabbage, carrots, bell peppers, scallions, and cilantro, dressed in

a tangy sesame ginger dressing. This vibrant salad is packed with texture and flavor, making it a refreshing side dish or light lunch option.

· Southwest Quinoa Salad with Avocado Lime Dressing: A hearty salad featuring protein-rich quinoa, black beans, corn, bell peppers, cherry tomatoes, and avocado, tossed in a creamy avocado lime dressing. This nutritious and flavorful salad is a meal in itself and is perfect for a quick and satisfying lunch or dinner.

Tips for Elevating the Flavor of Soups and Salads:

While soups and salads are delicious on their own, there are several tips and tricks you can use to elevate their flavor and take them to the next level.

· Use Homemade Broth: Whenever possible, use homemade broth or stock as the base for your soups. Homemade broth adds depth of flavor and richness that store-bought broths simply can't match.

· Toast Spices and Nuts: Toasting spices and nuts before adding them to your soups and salads enhances their flavor and aroma, bringing out their natural oils and intensifying their taste.

· Experiment with Fresh Herbs and Citrus Zest: Fresh herbs and citrus zest add brightness and freshness to soups and salads, enhancing their flavor and aroma. Experiment with different combinations to find the perfect balance of flavors.

· Incorporate Texture: Adding a variety of textures to your soups and salads, such as crunchy vegetables, creamy avocado, and toasted nuts or seeds, creates a more interesting and satisfying eating experience.

In the world of soups and salads, flavor is king. Whether you're craving a comforting bowl of soup on a chilly day or a refreshing salad on a hot summer afternoon, there's a world of flavor waiting to be explored. With hearty soups packed with flavorful ingredients, vibrant salads with creative dressings, and tips for elevating their flavor, you'll never be short on delicious options to tantalize your taste buds. So, let your culinary creativity soar as you embark on a flavorful journey of soups and salads bursting with flavor.

# CHAPTER 6: FLAVORFUL MAIN COURSES: FROM MEAT TO VEGETARIAN

Main courses serve as the centerpiece of any meal, offering a canvas for creativity and flavor exploration. In this chapter, we'll explore succulent meat dishes bursting with flavor, flavorful seafood creations that transport you to the coast, and creative vegetarian and vegan main courses that satisfy even the most discerning palates.

Succulent Meat Dishes Bursting with Flavor:

Meat dishes are the epitome of indulgence, offering rich, savory flavors and satisfying textures. From tender roasts to succulent braises, there's a meat dish to suit every taste and occasion.

- Beef Bourguignon: A classic French dish featuring tender beef stewed in red wine with aromatic vegetables, mushrooms, and herbs. This hearty and flavorful dish is perfect for special occasions and dinner parties, as it can be prepared in advance and reheated just before serving.
- Lemon Herb Roast Chicken: A simple yet elegant dish featuring a whole chicken marinated in a mixture of lemon juice, garlic, herbs, and olive oil, then roasted until golden and crispy. This succulent roast chicken is bursting with bright, fresh flavors and makes a delicious centerpiece for any meal.
- Spicy BBQ Ribs: Tender pork ribs coated in a smoky and spicy barbecue sauce, then slow-cooked until fall-off-the-bone tender. These finger-licking ribs are perfect for summer cookouts and backyard barbecues, where they're sure to be a hit with family and friends.

Flavorful Seafood Creations:
Seafood dishes offer a taste of the ocean, with their delicate flavors and briny freshness. From grilled fish to seafood pasta, there's a seafood creation to suit every palate and occasion.

- Grilled Salmon with Dill Sauce: Fresh salmon fillets marinated in a mixture of lemon juice, garlic, and herbs, then grilled to perfection and served with a creamy dill sauce. This elegant dish is bursting with flavor and pairs perfectly with a side of roasted vegetables or a crisp green salad.
- Shrimp Scampi with Linguine: Succulent shrimp cooked in a garlic and white wine sauce, then tossed with al dente linguine and finished with a squeeze of lemon

juice and a sprinkle of parsley. This classic Italian dish is quick and easy to prepare but packed with bold, vibrant flavors that will impress even the most discerning diners.

- Seafood Paella: A vibrant and flavorful Spanish dish featuring a colorful medley of seafood, including shrimp, mussels, and clams, cooked with saffron-infused rice, tomatoes, bell peppers, and peas. This hearty and satisfying dish is perfect for entertaining and is sure to transport your taste buds to the shores of Spain.

Creative Vegetarian and Vegan Main Courses:

Vegetarian and vegan main courses offer a world of flavor and creativity, with their emphasis on fresh, plant-based ingredients and bold seasoning. From hearty bean stews to innovative vegetable dishes, there's a vegetarian or vegan main course to satisfy every palate.

- Eggplant Parmesan: Tender slices of eggplant coated in breadcrumbs, fried until golden and crispy, then layered with marinara sauce and melted mozzarella cheese. This vegetarian twist on a classic Italian dish is bursting with flavor and perfect for meatless Mondays or a cozy weeknight dinner.
- Lentil Shepherd's Pie: Hearty lentil and vegetable filling topped with creamy mashed potatoes and baked until golden and bubbling. This vegan take on a traditional comfort food favorite is packed with protein, fiber, and flavor, making it a satisfying and nutritious meal for the whole family.

- Portobello Mushroom Steaks: Meaty portobello mushrooms marinated in balsamic vinegar, garlic, and herbs, then grilled until tender and juicy. These hearty mushroom steaks are a delicious and satisfying alternative to traditional meat dishes and are perfect for vegetarians and meat-eaters alike.

In the world of main courses, the possibilities are endless. Whether you're craving succulent meat dishes bursting with flavor, flavorful seafood creations that transport you to the coast, or creative vegetarian and vegan main courses that satisfy even the most discerning palates, there's a world of flavor waiting to be explored. So, let your culinary creativity shine as you embark on a flavorful journey of main courses that delight and inspire.

# CHAPTER 7: FLAVORFUL SIDES AND ACCOMPANIMENTS

---

Side dishes and accompaniments play a vital role in rounding out a meal, providing texture, flavor, and balance to the main course. In this chapter, we'll explore delicious side dishes to complement your main course, flavorful rice, grains, and pasta dishes that stand on their own, and creative ways to serve vegetables bursting with flavor.

Delicious Side Dishes to Complement Your Main Course:

Side dishes are the unsung heroes of the dining table, adding depth and variety to a meal while complementing the flavors of the main course. From roasted vegetables to creamy mashed potatoes, there's a side dish to suit every taste and occasion.

- Garlic Herb Roasted Potatoes: Crispy roasted potatoes tossed with garlic, olive oil, and a medley of fresh herbs, then baked until golden and fragrant. These flavorful potatoes make the perfect accompaniment to roasted meats, grilled fish, or vegetarian mains.

· Sauteed Green Beans with Almonds: Tender green beans sautéed with garlic, shallots, and toasted almonds, then finished with a squeeze of lemon juice and a sprinkle of fresh herbs. This simple yet elegant side dish adds a pop of color and freshness to any meal.

· Creamy Cauliflower Mash: A low-carb alternative to traditional mashed potatoes, made with steamed cauliflower blended with butter, cream, garlic, and Parmesan cheese until smooth and creamy. This decadent side dish is perfect for special occasions or as a comforting accompaniment to roasted meats or poultry.

Flavorful Rice, Grains, and Pasta Dishes:

Rice, grains, and pasta are versatile ingredients that serve as the perfect canvas for a wide range of flavors and textures. From fragrant rice pilafs to hearty grain salads, there's a dish to suit every taste and dietary preference.

· Lemon Herb Quinoa Salad: Nutty quinoa tossed with fresh herbs, lemon zest, toasted pine nuts, and dried cranberries, then dressed with a tangy vinaigrette. This vibrant and flavorful salad is perfect for summer picnics, potlucks, or as a light and refreshing side dish.

· Mushroom Risotto with Parmesan Cheese: Creamy risotto studded with earthy mushrooms, shallots, garlic, and Parmesan cheese, then finished with a drizzle of truffle oil and a sprinkle of fresh parsley. This indulgent dish is perfect for special occasions or as a comforting weeknight meal.

- Spaghetti Aglio e Olio: Simple yet satisfying spaghetti tossed with garlic-infused olive oil, red pepper flakes, and fresh parsley. This classic Italian dish is quick and easy to prepare but bursting with bold, vibrant flavors that will transport you to the streets of Rome with every bite.

Creative Ways to Serve Vegetables Bursting with Flavor:

Vegetables are the unsung heroes of the culinary world, offering a rainbow of colors, flavors, and textures that add vibrancy and freshness to any meal. From roasted root vegetables to crisp salads, there's no limit to the creative ways you can serve vegetables bursting with flavor.

- Grilled Vegetable Platter with Balsamic Glaze: A colorful assortment of seasonal vegetables, such as bell peppers, zucchini, eggplant, and cherry tomatoes, grilled to perfection and drizzled with a sweet and tangy balsamic glaze. This vibrant and flavorful dish is perfect for summer cookouts and backyard barbecues.
- Cauliflower Steak with Chimichurri Sauce: Thick slices of cauliflower roasted until tender and caramelized, then topped with a vibrant and herbaceous chimichurri sauce made with fresh parsley, cilantro, garlic, olive oil, and vinegar. This hearty and flavorful dish is perfect for vegetarians and meat-eaters alike.
- Kale Caesar Salad with Homemade Dressing: Nutrient-rich kale tossed with crisp romaine lettuce, garlic croutons, shaved Parmesan cheese, and a creamy homemade

Caesar dressing made with anchovies, garlic, lemon juice, Dijon mustard, and olive oil. This flavorful twist on a classic salad is both satisfying and nutritious.

In the world of side dishes and accompaniments, there's no shortage of delicious options to complement your main course and elevate your meal to new heights. Whether you're craving roasted vegetables, flavorful rice and grains, or creative ways to serve vegetables bursting with flavor, there's a world of culinary possibilities waiting to be explored. So, let your creativity shine as you experiment with new ingredients, flavors, and techniques to create side dishes that delight and inspire.

# CHAPTER 8: BAKING WITH FLAVOR: SWEET AND SAVORY TREATS

Baking is both an art and a science, where flavors meld and textures transform into delightful creations that tantalize the taste buds. In this chapter, we'll explore decadent desserts packed with flavor, flavorful breads, muffins, and pastries that comfort the soul, and tips for adding flavor to your baked goods to elevate them to new heights.

Decadent Desserts Packed with Flavor:

Desserts are the crowning glory of any meal, offering a sweet conclusion that leaves a lasting impression. From rich chocolate cakes to fruity tarts, there's a dessert to satisfy every craving and occasion.

- Chocolate Lava Cake with Raspberry Coulis: A decadent chocolate cake with a molten chocolate center, served with a tangy raspberry coulis and a dollop of whipped cream. This indulgent dessert is perfect for special occasions or as a romantic finale to a dinner for two.
- Tiramisu with Espresso Soaked Ladyfingers: A classic Italian dessert featuring layers of espresso-soaked ladyfingers, creamy mascarpone cheese, and a dusting of cocoa powder. This elegant and sophisticated dessert is sure to impress with its rich flavors and velvety texture.
- Lemon Blueberry Cheesecake Bars: Creamy cheesecake swirled with tangy lemon curd and studded with plump blueberries, all atop a buttery graham cracker crust. These irresistible bars strike the perfect balance between sweet and tart and are perfect for summer gatherings or afternoon tea.

Flavorful Breads, Muffins, and Pastries:

Breads, muffins, and pastries are comfort foods that warm the soul and fill the air with irresistible aromas. From crusty artisan loaves to tender scones, there's a baked treat to suit every taste and occasion.

- Rosemary Garlic Focaccia: A fragrant and flavorful focaccia bread topped with fresh rosemary, garlic, and coarse sea salt. This rustic Italian bread is perfect for tearing and sharing with friends and family, or for dipping into olive oil and balsamic vinegar as an appetizer.
- Blueberry Lemon Muffins with Streusel Topping: Tender muffins bursting with juicy blueberries and bright lemon zest, topped with a crunchy streusel topping made with

oats, brown sugar, and cinnamon. These irresistible muffins are perfect for breakfast, brunch, or as a midday snack.

· Spinach and Feta Cheese Puff Pastry Pinwheels: Flaky puff pastry filled with a savory mixture of spinach, feta cheese, garlic, and herbs, then rolled into pinwheels and baked until golden and crispy. These elegant and flavorful pastries are perfect for parties, picnics, or as a light lunch or appetizer.

Tips for Adding Flavor to Your Baked Goods:

While baking is a precise science, there are several tips and tricks you can use to add flavor to your baked goods and take them to the next level.

· Use Quality Ingredients: The quality of your ingredients can make a significant difference in the flavor of your baked goods. Use fresh, high-quality ingredients whenever possible, including real butter, pure vanilla extract, and fresh herbs and spices.

· Experiment with Flavorful Add-Ins: Get creative with add-ins like chocolate chips, nuts, dried fruit, and spices to add depth and complexity to your baked goods. Consider combining unexpected flavor combinations, such as chocolate and chili, or cinnamon and cardamom, for a unique twist on classic recipes.

· Enhance Aromas with Extracts and Zests: Extracts such as almond, citrus, and mint can add subtle yet impactful flavors to your baked goods, while citrus zests can add brightness and freshness. Experiment with different extracts and zests to find the perfect balance of flavors for your recipes.

· Don't Forget About Seasonings: Just like savory dishes, baked goods can benefit from the addition of seasonings such as cinnamon, nutmeg, ginger, and cardamom. These warm spices add depth and warmth to your baked goods and can transform a simple recipe into a memorable treat.

In the world of baking, flavor is king. Whether you're whipping up decadent desserts packed with flavor, flavorful breads, muffins, and pastries that comfort the soul, or experimenting with tips for adding flavor to your baked goods, there's a world of culinary possibilities waiting to be explored. So, let your creativity shine as you mix, knead, and bake your way to delicious delights that delight and inspire.

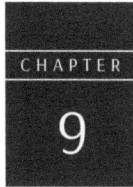

# CHAPTER 9: DRINKS AND BEVERAGES: FLAVORFUL REFRESHMENTS

Drinks and beverages are not just thirst-quenchers; they're opportunities to indulge in a symphony of flavors. In this chapter, we'll explore flavorful cocktails and mocktails that delight the senses, refreshing beverages bursting with flavor, and creative ways to infuse flavor into your drinks to elevate any occasion.

Flavorful Cocktails and Mocktails:

Cocktails and mocktails are a celebration of flavor, combining a variety of ingredients to create complex and satisfying beverages. Whether you prefer something with a kick or a non-alcoholic option, there's a cocktail or mocktail to suit every taste and occasion.

- Classic Mojito: A refreshing cocktail made with white rum, fresh mint leaves, lime juice, simple syrup, and club soda. This iconic Cuban drink is bursting with bright, citrusy flavors and is perfect for sipping on a hot summer day.
- Virgin Strawberry Daiquiri: A non-alcoholic version of the classic daiquiri made with fresh strawberries, lime juice, simple syrup, and ice. This fruity and refreshing mocktail is perfect for guests of all ages and can be enjoyed any time of year.
- Spicy Margarita: A bold and flavorful cocktail made with tequila, lime juice, triple sec, and a splash of jalapeno-infused simple syrup. This fiery twist on the classic margarita is perfect for those who like a little heat in their drinks.

Refreshing Beverages Bursting with Flavor:

From fruit-infused waters to herbal teas, refreshing beverages offer a burst of flavor and hydration that quenches the thirst and invigorates the senses. Whether enjoyed hot or cold, there's a refreshing beverage to suit every mood and occasion.

- Cucumber Mint Infused Water: Cool and refreshing water infused with slices of cucumber and sprigs of fresh mint. This hydrating beverage is perfect for hot summer days and adds a subtle yet refreshing flavor to plain water.
- Iced Green Tea with Citrus: Chilled green tea infused with slices of lemon, lime, and orange, sweetened with a touch of honey or agave syrup. This antioxidant-rich

beverage is perfect for cooling off on a hot day and provides a refreshing burst of citrus flavor.

- Hibiscus Ginger Cooler: A tart and tangy beverage made
  with brewed hibiscus tea, fresh ginger, and a splash of
  sparkling water. This invigorating cooler is bursting with
  tropical flavors and is perfect for sipping on a sunny
  afternoon.

Creative Ways to Infuse Flavor into Your Drinks:

Infusing flavor into drinks is a fun and creative way to
elevate their taste and appeal. From fresh herbs and spices to
fruit purees and floral extracts, there are countless ways to
add depth and complexity to your beverages.

- Herb-Infused Simple Syrups: Make your own flavored
  simple syrups by simmering sugar, water, and your
  choice of herbs or spices, such as rosemary, basil, or
  cinnamon. These infused syrups can be used to sweeten
  cocktails, mocktails, and other beverages, adding a subtle yet distinctive flavor.
- Fruit and Vegetable Juices: Freshly squeezed fruit and
  vegetable juices are a natural way to infuse flavor into
  your drinks. Experiment with different combinations of
  fruits and vegetables to create refreshing and nutritious
  beverages that are bursting with flavor.
- Floral Waters and Extracts: Floral waters and extracts,
  such as rose water, orange blossom water, and lavender
  extract, add a delicate floral aroma and flavor to beverages. Use them sparingly to add a subtle yet sophisticated touch to cocktails, mocktails, and other drinks.

In the world of drinks and beverages, flavor is key. Whether you're indulging in flavorful cocktails and mocktails, refreshing beverages bursting with flavor, or exploring creative ways to infuse flavor into your drinks, there's a world of culinary possibilities waiting to be explored. So, let your taste buds be your guide as you mix, shake, and stir your way to delicious refreshments that delight and inspire.

# CHAPTER 10: FUSION FLAVORS: EXPLORING GLOBAL CUISINE

Global cuisine offers a rich tapestry of flavors, ingredients, and culinary techniques that inspire creativity and innovation in the kitchen. In this chapter, we'll explore flavorful recipes inspired by different cultures, delve into the world of fusion cuisine and flavor pairings, and discover tips for incorporating global flavors into your cooking to create dishes that tantalize the taste buds and transport you to distant lands.

Flavorful Recipes Inspired by Different Cultures:

Every culture has its own unique culinary traditions and signature dishes that reflect its history, geography, and cultural heritage. By drawing inspiration from diverse cuisines, you can create flavorful recipes that pay homage to these rich culinary traditions while putting your own spin on them.

- Thai Green Curry with Coconut Rice: Fragrant and aromatic Thai green curry made with a homemade curry paste, tender chicken or tofu, coconut milk, and a variety of vegetables, served with fluffy coconut rice. This vibrant and flavorful dish captures the essence of Thai cuisine and is perfect for a weeknight dinner or special occasion.
- Mexican Street Corn Salad (Esquites): A zesty and refreshing salad inspired by the flavors of Mexican street food, featuring charred corn kernels tossed with mayonnaise, lime juice, chili powder, cotija cheese, and cilantro. This tangy and flavorful salad is perfect for summer cookouts and backyard barbecues.
- Indian Butter Chicken (Murgh Makhani): A rich and creamy Indian dish featuring tender chicken simmered in a velvety tomato-based sauce infused with butter, cream, and aromatic spices, served with fluffy basmati rice and warm naan bread. This indulgent and flavorful dish is a favorite in Indian restaurants around the world.

Exploring Fusion Cuisine and Flavor Pairings:

Fusion cuisine is the art of blending culinary traditions and ingredients from different cultures to create innovative and exciting dishes that push the boundaries of traditional cooking. By combining unexpected flavor pairings and techniques, you can create dishes that are both familiar and exotic, comforting and adventurous.

- Korean BBQ Tacos: A fusion twist on classic Korean BBQ, featuring tender marinated beef or tofu wrapped in warm corn tortillas and topped with crunchy slaw, kimchi, and a drizzle of spicy gochujang sauce. These flavorful tacos combine the bold flavors of Korean cuisine with the familiar comfort of Mexican street food.

· Sushi Burrito: A playful fusion of Japanese sushi and Mexican burritos, featuring a giant seaweed wrap filled with sushi rice, fresh sashimi or cooked seafood, avocado, cucumber, and other colorful vegetables, all rolled up into a portable and flavorful meal. This innovative dish is perfect for on-the-go dining or picnics in the park.

· Moroccan Spiced Lamb Burgers: A fusion of North African and Western flavors, featuring juicy lamb burgers seasoned with aromatic Moroccan spices such as cumin, coriander, cinnamon, and paprika, served on toasted brioche buns with harissa aioli, caramelized onions, and feta cheese. These flavorful burgers are sure to be a hit at your next barbecue or dinner party.

Tips for Incorporating Global Flavors into Your Cooking:

Incorporating global flavors into your cooking is a fun and rewarding way to expand your culinary repertoire and create dishes that are as diverse and flavorful as the world itself. Here are some tips for incorporating global flavors into your cooking:

· Experiment with Spices and Seasonings: Stock your pantry with a variety of spices and seasonings from around the world, such as curry powder, garam masala, za'atar, and five-spice powder, and experiment with different combinations to create unique flavor profiles.

· Try New Ingredients: Be adventurous and try new ingredients from different cultures, such as miso paste, tamarind, coconut milk, and kimchi, to add depth and complexity to your dishes.

- Learn from Different Cuisines: Take inspiration from different cuisines by exploring cookbooks, watching cooking shows, and dining at ethnic restaurants. Pay attention to flavor combinations, cooking techniques, and presentation styles, and incorporate what you learn into your own cooking.
- Embrace Creativity: Don't be afraid to think outside the box and get creative with your cooking. Combine ingredients and techniques from different cultures to create dishes that are uniquely yours and reflect your own culinary journey.

In the world of fusion flavors and global cuisine, the possibilities are endless. By drawing inspiration from diverse culinary traditions, exploring fusion cuisine and flavor pairings, and incorporating global flavors into your cooking, you can create dishes that are as exciting and flavorful as they are delicious. So, let your taste buds be your guide as you embark on a culinary adventure that spans the globe and celebrates the rich tapestry of flavors that unite us all.

# CHAPTER 11: COOKING WITH SEASONAL AND LOCAL INGREDIENTS

Cooking with seasonal and local ingredients is not only a culinary choice but also a lifestyle that promotes sustainability, freshness, and flavor. In this chapter, we'll explore the importance of seasonal and local ingredients, share flavorful recipes using seasonal produce, and offer tips for shopping for and cooking with seasonal ingredients to maximize their taste and nutritional benefits.

The Importance of Seasonal and Local Ingredients:

Seasonal and local ingredients are those that are harvested at their peak ripeness and freshness, typically grown within a certain radius of where they are sold. Choosing seasonal and local ingredients offers numerous benefits, both for your health and the environment:

- Fresher Flavor: Seasonal ingredients are harvested at their peak ripeness, meaning they are bursting with flavor and nutritional goodness. By cooking with seasonal ingredients, you can enjoy the true essence of each ingredient and enhance the overall taste of your dishes.
- Nutritional Benefits: Seasonal ingredients are often more nutritious than their out-of-season counterparts, as they are allowed to fully develop their nutrients and antioxidants before being harvested. By incorporating seasonal produce into your diet, you can boost your intake of vitamins, minerals, and other essential nutrients.
- Support for Local Farmers: Choosing local ingredients supports small-scale farmers and producers in your community, helping to strengthen local economies and preserve agricultural traditions. By purchasing directly from farmers markets or joining a community-supported agriculture (CSA) program, you can establish a closer connection to the people who grow your food and gain a greater appreciation for the effort that goes into producing it.

Flavorful Recipes Using Seasonal Produce:

Cooking with seasonal produce allows you to take advantage of the natural bounty of each season, creating dishes that are fresh, vibrant, and full of flavor. Here are some delicious recipes that showcase the best of seasonal ingredients:

- Summer Caprese Salad: A classic Italian salad featuring ripe tomatoes, fresh mozzarella cheese, and fragrant basil leaves, drizzled with balsamic glaze and extra virgin olive oil. This simple yet elegant dish celebrates the flavors of summer and makes a perfect appetizer or light meal.

- Autumn Butternut Squash Soup: A comforting soup made with roasted butternut squash, caramelized onions, and aromatic spices such as cinnamon, nutmeg, and cloves, finished with a swirl of creamy coconut milk. This cozy soup is perfect for warming up on chilly autumn evenings and pairs beautifully with crusty bread or a simple salad.
- Spring Asparagus and Pea Risotto: A creamy risotto made with Arborio rice, tender asparagus spears, sweet peas, and fragrant herbs such as parsley and lemon zest. This vibrant dish captures the fresh flavors of spring and makes a satisfying main course or side dish for any occasion.

Tips for Shopping for and Cooking with Seasonal Ingredients:

Shopping for and cooking with seasonal ingredients can be a rewarding and enjoyable experience, but it requires some planning and knowledge of what's in season. Here are some tips to help you make the most of seasonal produce:

- Visit Farmers Markets: Farmers markets are a great place to find fresh, seasonal produce directly from local farmers. Take a stroll through your local farmers market and explore the variety of fruits, vegetables, and other products available. Chat with the farmers and ask for recommendations on how to cook and enjoy their seasonal offerings.

- Plan Your Meals Around Seasonal Ingredients: When meal planning, take into account what's in season and plan your meals accordingly. Look for recipes that highlight seasonal produce and incorporate them into your weekly menu. This will not only ensure that you're cooking with the freshest ingredients but also help you discover new flavors and culinary combinations.
- Preserve the Harvest: To enjoy the flavors of seasonal produce year-round, consider preserving the harvest through methods such as canning, freezing, drying, or pickling. This allows you to enjoy your favorite seasonal ingredients even when they're out of season and adds variety to your meals throughout the year.
- Experiment with Different Cooking Techniques: Seasonal ingredients lend themselves to a variety of cooking techniques, from grilling and roasting to sautéing and steaming. Experiment with different methods to bring out the best flavors and textures in your seasonal dishes and keep your meals interesting and exciting.

Cooking with seasonal and local ingredients is a delicious and sustainable way to connect with the natural world and enjoy the flavors of each season. By understanding the importance of seasonal ingredients, exploring flavorful recipes using seasonal produce, and following tips for shopping for and cooking with seasonal ingredients, you can create dishes that are not only delicious but also nourishing for your body and soul. So, embrace the bounty of each season and let it inspire you to cook with creativity, passion, and flavor.

# CHAPTER 12: COOKING TECHNIQUES FOR MAXIMUM FLAVOR

Mastering cooking techniques is essential for unlocking the full potential of ingredients and creating dishes that are bursting with flavor. In this chapter, we'll explore different cooking methods and their impact on flavor, share tips for searing, grilling, roasting, and braising to enhance flavor, and discuss how to lock in flavor when cooking to ensure that every dish you create is a culinary delight.

Exploring Different Cooking Methods and Their Impact on Flavor:

Each cooking method brings its own unique set of flavors and textures to the table, resulting in dishes that are distinct and memorable. By understanding the characteristics of different cooking methods, you can choose the right technique to enhance the flavor of your ingredients and elevate your dishes to new heights.

- Searing: Searing involves cooking food at high heat in a dry pan or on a grill to create a caramelized crust on the exterior, locking in moisture and enhancing flavor. This technique is ideal for meats, fish, and vegetables, imparting a rich, savory flavor and appealing texture.
- Grilling: Grilling imparts a smoky, charred flavor to food, thanks to direct exposure to an open flame or hot grill grates. Whether you're grilling steaks, vegetables, or even fruits, this technique adds depth and complexity to dishes and creates a satisfying contrast between crispy exterior and tender interior.
- Roasting: Roasting involves cooking food in an oven at a high temperature, allowing the natural sugars to caramelize and develop rich, complex flavors. This technique is perfect for meats, poultry, root vegetables, and even fruits, resulting in dishes that are tender, juicy, and bursting with flavor.
- Braising: Braising involves cooking food slowly in a flavorful liquid, such as broth, wine, or sauce, at a low temperature, allowing the ingredients to tenderize and absorb the rich flavors of the cooking liquid. This technique is well-suited for tough cuts of meat, vegetables, and legumes, resulting in dishes that are succulent, aromatic, and deeply satisfying.

Tips for Searing, Grilling, Roasting, and Braising:

To achieve maximum flavor when searing, grilling, roasting, and braising, it's essential to follow a few key tips and techniques:

- Preheat Your Cooking Surface: Before you begin cooking, make sure your pan, grill, or oven is thoroughly preheated to ensure even cooking and optimal flavor development.
- Use High-Quality Ingredients: Start with the freshest, highest-quality ingredients available to maximize flavor and ensure the best possible results.
- Season Generously: Don't be afraid to season your ingredients generously with salt, pepper, herbs, and spices to enhance their natural flavors and create depth of flavor in your dishes.
- Control Your Cooking Temperature: Pay attention to your cooking temperature and adjust it as needed to prevent burning or undercooking your food and achieve perfect results every time.
- Rest Your Meat: Allow meat to rest for a few minutes after cooking to allow the juices to redistribute and ensure that it remains tender and juicy.

How to Lock in Flavor When Cooking:

Locking in flavor when cooking is essential for creating dishes that are flavorful, juicy, and satisfying. Here are some tips for preserving and enhancing flavor during the cooking process:

- Start with a Hot Pan: When searing or sautéing ingredients, start with a hot pan to create a golden brown crust and seal in the natural juices and flavors.
- Use Marinades and Rubs: Marinating meat, poultry, or seafood in a flavorful marinade or rub before cooking can infuse it with additional flavor and enhance its taste and texture.
- Add Aromatics: Enhance the flavor of your dishes by adding aromatics such as onions, garlic, ginger, and fresh herbs to the cooking process. These aromatic ingredients add depth and complexity to dishes and create a rich, flavorful base for sauces, soups, and stews.
- Deglaze the Pan: After cooking meat or vegetables, deglaze the pan with wine, broth, or other liquid to capture the flavorful browned bits and incorporate them into sauces, gravies, or glazes.
- Finish with Fresh Ingredients: Add a final burst of flavor to your dishes by finishing them with fresh herbs, citrus zest, or a drizzle of high-quality olive oil. These finishing touches can elevate the flavor of your dishes and create a memorable dining experience.

By mastering cooking techniques such as searing, grilling, roasting, and braising, and following tips for locking in flavor when cooking, you can create dishes that are bursting with flavor and guaranteed to impress. So, let your culinary creativity shine as you explore the world of cooking techniques and unleash the full potential of your ingredients to create dishes that delight the senses and nourish the soul.

# CHAPTER 13: PRESENTATION AND PLATING: ENHANCING THE FLAVOR EXPERIENCE

Presentation is not just about making your dishes look beautiful; it's also about enhancing the overall flavor experience for the diner. In this chapter, we'll explore the importance of presentation in cooking, share tips for plating your dishes for maximum flavor impact, and discuss creative garnishes and finishing touches that elevate the dining experience to new heights.

The Importance of Presentation in Cooking:

Presentation plays a crucial role in how we perceive and enjoy food. A well-presented dish not only stimulates the appetite but also enhances the overall dining experience by engaging multiple senses. Here's why presentation is important in cooking:

- Visual Appeal: The first impression of a dish is visual, and a beautifully presented plate immediately captivates the diner's attention and sets the stage for the flavor experience to come.
- Appetite Stimulation: A visually appealing presentation stimulates the appetite and increases anticipation, making the diner more receptive to the flavors and aromas of the dish.
- Balance and Harmony: Thoughtful plating creates a sense of balance and harmony on the plate, ensuring that each component complements the others and contributes to the overall flavor profile of the dish.

Tips for Plating Your Dishes for Maximum Flavor Impact:

Plating is an art form that requires careful attention to detail and a keen eye for composition. Here are some tips for plating your dishes to maximize flavor impact and create a memorable dining experience:

- Consider Color and Texture: Choose ingredients with vibrant colors and contrasting textures to create visual interest and enhance the overall flavor experience. Think about how different colors and textures will play off each other on the plate and use them to create a visually appealing composition.
- Use Negative Space: Leave empty space on the plate to allow the individual components of the dish to stand out and shine. Negative space not only adds visual interest but also helps to create a sense of balance and harmony on the plate.

- Plate with Purpose: Be intentional about how you arrange the components of the dish on the plate, considering both aesthetics and practicality. Arrange ingredients in a way that guides the diner's eye around the plate and highlights the focal point of the dish.
- Pay Attention to Proportions: Balance is key when plating a dish, so pay attention to the proportions of each component and ensure that they are harmoniously arranged on the plate. Avoid overcrowding the plate and strive for a clean, elegant presentation.

Creative Garnishes and Finishing Touches:

Garnishes and finishing touches add the final layer of flavor and visual appeal to a dish, elevating it from good to exceptional. Here are some creative garnishes and finishing touches to consider:

- Fresh Herbs: Sprinkle chopped fresh herbs over the top of the dish to add brightness and freshness and enhance the flavor profile.
- Citrus Zest: Use a microplane grater to zest citrus fruits such as lemon, lime, or orange over the dish to add a burst of citrusy flavor and aroma.
- Edible Flowers: Garnish the dish with edible flowers such as nasturtiums, pansies, or violets to add a pop of color and a delicate floral aroma.
- Drizzles and Sauces: Use a squeeze bottle to drizzle sauces or flavored oils onto the plate in an artistic manner, adding depth and complexity to the dish.

- Crispy Toppings: Add a crunchy element to the dish by sprinkling crispy toppings such as toasted nuts, seeds, or breadcrumbs over the top.

By paying attention to presentation and plating, and incorporating creative garnishes and finishing touches, you can enhance the flavor experience and create dishes that are as visually stunning as they are delicious. So, let your creativity shine as you explore the art of plating and elevate your culinary creations to new heights of flavor and elegance.

# CHAPTER 14: COOKING WITH FLAVOR ON A BUDGET

Cooking flavorful meals doesn't have to break the bank. In this chapter, we'll explore budget-friendly ingredients packed with flavor, share tips for maximizing flavor without breaking the bank, and provide affordable recipes bursting with deliciousness.

Budget-Friendly Ingredients Packed with Flavor:

Delicious meals can be created using affordable ingredients that are full of flavor. Here are some budget-friendly ingredients to consider:

- Beans and Legumes: Beans and legumes, such as black beans, lentils, and chickpeas, are not only affordable but also versatile and nutritious. They add texture, protein, and flavor to dishes like soups, stews, salads, and dips.

- Root Vegetables: Root vegetables like potatoes, carrots, onions, and beets are inexpensive staples that can be used in a variety of dishes. Roast them, mash them, or add them to soups and casseroles for hearty and flavorful meals.
- Canned Tomatoes: Canned tomatoes are a pantry staple that adds depth and richness to sauces, soups, stews, and casseroles. They're affordable, convenient, and packed with flavor, making them a great option for budget-friendly cooking.
- Whole Grains: Whole grains such as rice, quinoa, barley, and oats are not only nutritious but also affordable. They can be used as a base for dishes like pilafs, stir-fries, salads, and soups, adding texture and flavor to your meals.
- Herbs and Spices: Herbs and spices are a cost-effective way to add flavor to your dishes without adding extra calories or sodium. Stock your pantry with essentials like garlic powder, onion powder, cumin, paprika, and dried herbs like oregano, thyme, and rosemary.

Tips for Maximizing Flavor without Breaking the Bank:

Creating flavorful meals on a budget requires some creativity and planning. Here are some tips for maximizing flavor without breaking the bank:

- Shop Seasonally: Purchase fruits and vegetables that are in season, as they tend to be more affordable and flavorful. Visit farmers markets or look for sales and discounts at your local grocery store to find the best deals on fresh produce.

- Buy in Bulk: Purchase pantry staples like grains, beans, legumes, and spices in bulk to save money and reduce waste. Buying in bulk often allows you to get more bang for your buck and ensures that you always have essential ingredients on hand for cooking flavorful meals.
- Use Leftovers Wisely: Don't let leftovers go to waste! Repurpose leftover ingredients into new dishes, such as soups, salads, stir-fries, casseroles, or sandwiches. Get creative and experiment with different flavor combinations to create delicious meals using what you already have on hand.
- Cook from Scratch: Cooking from scratch is often more affordable than buying pre-packaged or convenience foods, and it allows you to control the ingredients and flavors in your meals. Invest in basic cooking skills and techniques to create homemade dishes that are flavorful, nutritious, and budget-friendly.

Affordable Recipes Bursting with Flavor:

Creating flavorful meals on a budget is easier than you might think. Here are some affordable recipes bursting with flavor to inspire your next budget-friendly meal:

- Vegetable Stir-Fry: A colorful and vibrant stir-fry made with an assortment of fresh vegetables like bell peppers, broccoli, carrots, and snap peas, sautéed with garlic, ginger, soy sauce, and a touch of honey or brown sugar for sweetness. Serve over cooked rice or noodles for a satisfying and budget-friendly meal.
- Black Bean and Sweet Potato Chili: A hearty and nutritious chili made with black beans, sweet potatoes,

onions, bell peppers, tomatoes, and a blend of spices like chili powder, cumin, and paprika. Simmer until thick and flavorful, then serve topped with shredded cheese, chopped cilantro, and a dollop of Greek yogurt or sour cream.

· Lentil and Vegetable Curry: A fragrant and comforting curry made with lentils, cauliflower, carrots, onions, and tomatoes, simmered in a flavorful coconut milk-based sauce infused with curry spices like turmeric, cumin, coriander, and ginger. Serve over cooked rice or quinoa for a satisfying and budget-friendly meal.

· Tomato Basil Pasta: A simple yet delicious pasta dish made with spaghetti or your favorite pasta shape, tossed with a homemade tomato basil sauce made with canned tomatoes, garlic, onions, and fresh basil. Top with grated Parmesan cheese and a drizzle of extra virgin olive oil for a quick and budget-friendly meal.

By using budget-friendly ingredients, following tips for maximizing flavor without breaking the bank, and trying out affordable recipes bursting with flavor, you can enjoy delicious and satisfying meals without straining your wallet. So, roll up your sleeves, get creative in the kitchen, and discover the joy of cooking flavorful meals on a budget.

# CHAPTER 15: FLAVORFUL COOKING FOR SPECIAL DIETARY NEEDS

Cooking for special dietary needs doesn't mean sacrificing flavor. In this chapter, we'll explore flavorful recipes tailored for various dietary restrictions, including gluten-free diets, dairy-free lifestyles, and special diets like Paleo and Keto. These recipes prove that delicious and satisfying meals can be enjoyed by everyone, regardless of dietary requirements.

Flavorful Recipes for Gluten-Free Diets:

For those following a gluten-free diet due to celiac disease or gluten sensitivity, it's important to find delicious alternatives that don't compromise on flavor. Here are some flavorful recipes that are naturally gluten-free:

- Quinoa Salad with Roasted Vegetables: A colorful and nutritious salad featuring fluffy quinoa, roasted vegetables (such as bell peppers, zucchini, and cherry tomatoes), fresh herbs, and a tangy lemon vinaigrette. This gluten-free dish is perfect for lunch or as a side dish for dinner.
- Grilled Lemon Garlic Chicken: Tender chicken breasts marinated in a mixture of lemon juice, garlic, olive oil, and herbs, then grilled to perfection. This flavorful and protein-packed dish pairs well with roasted vegetables or a simple green salad.
- Thai Peanut Noodles with Vegetables: A satisfying and flavorful noodle dish made with rice noodles, crunchy vegetables (such as bell peppers, carrots, and snow peas), and a creamy peanut sauce infused with Thai spices and flavors. Garnish with chopped peanuts and fresh cilantro for an extra burst of flavor.

Delicious Dishes for Dairy-Free Lifestyles:

For individuals with lactose intolerance or dairy allergies, cooking without dairy products doesn't mean sacrificing flavor or richness. Here are some delicious dairy-free recipes to enjoy:

- Coconut Curry Lentil Soup: A comforting and aromatic soup made with red lentils, coconut milk, tomatoes, onions, garlic, and a blend of Indian spices like cumin, coriander, and turmeric. Serve with a dollop of dairy-free yogurt or a sprinkle of fresh cilantro for added flavor.
- Dairy-Free Pesto Pasta: A vibrant and flavorful pasta dish featuring gluten-free pasta (such as brown rice or chickpea pasta) tossed with homemade dairy-free pesto

made with fresh basil, garlic, pine nuts, nutritional yeast, and olive oil. Top with cherry tomatoes and roasted vegetables for extra texture and flavor.

- Spicy Black Bean Tacos with Avocado Salsa: Flavorful black bean tacos topped with a zesty avocado salsa made with diced avocado, tomatoes, red onion, jalapeno, cilantro, and lime juice. Serve in gluten-free corn tortillas with a squeeze of fresh lime juice for a refreshing and satisfying meal.

Flavorful Cooking for Paleo, Keto, and Other Special Diets:

Special diets like Paleo and Keto focus on whole foods and specific macronutrient ratios while avoiding certain ingredients like grains, legumes, and added sugars. Here are some flavorful recipes tailored for these diets:

- Paleo Balsamic Glazed Salmon: Succulent salmon fillets marinated in a sweet and tangy balsamic glaze made with balsamic vinegar, honey (or maple syrup), garlic, and Dijon mustard, then baked or grilled to perfection. Serve with roasted vegetables or a side salad for a nutritious and satisfying meal.
- Keto Cauliflower Fried Rice: A low-carb and flavorful alternative to traditional fried rice made with riced cauliflower, scrambled eggs, diced vegetables, and a savory sauce made with coconut aminos, sesame oil, and garlic. This satisfying dish is packed with flavor and perfect for anyone following a Keto lifestyle.
- Vegan Cauliflower Pizza Crust: A grain-free and vegan alternative to traditional pizza crust made with cauliflower, ground flaxseeds, almond flour, and Italian herbs.

Top with dairy-free cheese, your favorite vegetables, and a drizzle of olive oil for a delicious and satisfying pizza that's both Paleo and Keto-friendly.

Cooking for special dietary needs doesn't have to be boring or bland. By exploring flavorful recipes tailored for gluten-free diets, dairy-free lifestyles, and special diets like Paleo and Keto, you can enjoy delicious and satisfying meals that meet your nutritional requirements and tantalize your taste buds. So, get creative in the kitchen, experiment with new ingredients and flavors, and discover the joy of flavorful cooking for special dietary needs.

# CHAPTER 16: COOKING WITH FLAVOR FOR HEALTH AND WELLNESS

Cooking with flavor doesn't have to mean sacrificing health and wellness. In fact, flavorful meals can be packed with nutrient-rich ingredients that nourish the body and support overall wellbeing. In this chapter, we'll explore flavorful recipes packed with nutrient-rich ingredients, share tips for cooking flavorful meals that are also healthy, and delve into the connection between flavor and wellbeing.

Flavorful Recipes Packed with Nutrient-Rich Ingredients:

Nutrient-rich ingredients are essential for promoting health and vitality. Here are some flavorful recipes that are not only delicious but also packed with essential nutrients:

- Mediterranean Quinoa Salad: A vibrant and nutritious salad featuring fluffy quinoa, cherry tomatoes, cucumbers, Kalamata olives, red onion, feta cheese (or dairy-free alternative), and a tangy lemon vinaigrette. This flavorful dish is packed with fiber, protein, vitamins, and minerals, making it a perfect choice for a light and satisfying meal.
- Salmon and Avocado Sushi Bowls: A nourishing and flavorful bowl featuring sushi-grade salmon, creamy avocado, cucumber, shredded carrots, nori strips, and sushi rice (or cauliflower rice for a low-carb option), drizzled with a homemade spicy mayo sauce. This nutrient-rich dish is packed with omega-3 fatty acids, protein, and antioxidants, making it a delicious and satisfying option for lunch or dinner.
- Roasted Vegetable Buddha Bowl: A colorful and nutrient-packed bowl featuring roasted vegetables (such as sweet potatoes, Brussels sprouts, cauliflower, and carrots), quinoa, chickpeas, avocado, and a creamy tahini dressing. This flavorful dish is rich in fiber, vitamins, and minerals, making it a satisfying and nourishing option for a healthy meal.

Tips for Cooking Flavorful Meals That Are Also Healthy:
Cooking flavorful meals that are also healthy requires some planning and creativity. Here are some tips to help you achieve both:

- Focus on Whole Foods: Choose whole, minimally processed ingredients like fruits, vegetables, whole grains, lean proteins, and healthy fats to create flavorful meals that are also nutritious and satisfying.

- Experiment with Herbs and Spices: Use herbs, spices, and aromatics to add flavor to your dishes without relying on excess salt, sugar, or unhealthy fats. Experiment with different combinations of herbs and spices to create unique flavor profiles that excite the taste buds and enhance the overall dining experience.
- Incorporate Plenty of Color: Aim to include a variety of colorful fruits and vegetables in your meals to ensure a diverse range of nutrients and flavors. The more colors you have on your plate, the more likely you are to get a wide array of vitamins, minerals, and antioxidants that support overall health and wellbeing.
- Practice Mindful Eating: Pay attention to your body's hunger and fullness cues, and savor each bite of your meal to fully appreciate the flavors and textures. Eating mindfully can help you enjoy your food more, prevent overeating, and foster a healthier relationship with food.

Exploring the Connection Between Flavor and Wellbeing:

The connection between flavor and wellbeing goes beyond just satisfying hunger; it encompasses the sensory experience of eating and the pleasure it brings. When we eat flavorful and satisfying meals, we not only nourish our bodies but also nourish our minds and souls.

- Mental Health Benefits: Eating flavorful meals can have a positive impact on mental health and wellbeing by reducing stress, boosting mood, and promoting feelings of happiness and satisfaction. When we enjoy delicious and satisfying food, it can lift our spirits and improve our overall outlook on life.

· Physical Health Benefits: Consuming nutrient-rich foods that are packed with flavor can support overall physical health and wellbeing by providing essential vitamins, minerals, antioxidants, and phytonutrients that promote optimal functioning of the body. Eating a balanced diet that includes a variety of flavorful foods can help prevent chronic diseases, support immune function, and maintain a healthy weight.

· Social and Emotional Benefits: Sharing flavorful meals with family and friends can strengthen social connections and foster a sense of community and belonging. Breaking bread together is a universal ritual that brings people together, sparks conversation, and creates lasting memories that contribute to overall wellbeing.

By cooking flavorful meals packed with nutrient-rich ingredients, following tips for cooking healthy and flavorful dishes, and exploring the connection between flavor and wellbeing, you can nourish your body, mind, and soul and enjoy a happier, healthier life. So, embrace the joy of cooking, savor the flavors of each meal, and reap the rewards of a flavorful and fulfilling lifestyle.

# CHAPTER 17: THE ART OF FLAVOR PAIRING

Mastering the art of flavor pairing is essential for creating dishes that are harmonious, balanced, and bursting with deliciousness. In this chapter, we'll delve into the principles of flavor affinities and combinations, explore how to pair ingredients for maximum flavor impact, and provide tips for experimenting with flavor pairings in your cooking to elevate your culinary creations to new heights.

Understanding Flavor Affinities and Combinations:

Flavor pairing is the art of combining ingredients that complement and enhance each other's flavors, creating a harmonious and balanced dish. Understanding flavor affinities and combinations is key to unlocking the full potential of ingredients and creating memorable culinary experiences. Here are some common flavor affinities and combinations to consider:

- Sweet and Savory: The combination of sweet and savory flavors creates a pleasing contrast that tantalizes the taste buds. Think of dishes like teriyaki chicken with a sweet and savory glaze, or caramelized onions paired with savory meats.
- Acidic and Rich: Acidic ingredients like citrus, vinegar, and tomatoes add brightness and freshness to rich and indulgent dishes, balancing out their richness and adding depth of flavor. Try adding a squeeze of lemon juice to creamy pasta dishes or a splash of balsamic vinegar to roasted vegetables.
- Spicy and Sweet: The combination of spicy and sweet flavors creates a dynamic and exciting taste experience. Think of dishes like spicy Thai curry with coconut milk and sweet mango, or spicy chili paired with a drizzle of honey or maple syrup.

Pairing Ingredients for Maximum Flavor Impact:

When pairing ingredients for maximum flavor impact, it's important to consider the unique characteristics of each ingredient and how they interact with each other. Here are some tips for pairing ingredients to create flavorful dishes:

- Consider Flavor Profiles: Choose ingredients that have complementary flavor profiles and textures to create a balanced and harmonious dish. For example, pair salty ingredients with sweet or acidic ones to create contrast and balance.
- Think about Textures: Consider the textures of the ingredients you're pairing and how they will contribute to the overall mouthfeel of the dish. Combining crispy,

crunchy elements with creamy or tender components can create a satisfying contrast that enhances the dining experience.

· Experiment with Contrasting Flavors: Don't be afraid to experiment with contrasting flavors and unexpected pairings to create dishes that are unique and memorable. Sometimes the most unlikely combinations can result in the most delicious surprises.

Tips for Experimenting with Flavor Pairings in Your Cooking:

Experimenting with flavor pairings is a fun and creative way to expand your culinary repertoire and discover new flavor combinations that excite the palate. Here are some tips for experimenting with flavor pairings in your cooking:

· Start with Small Batches: When experimenting with new flavor pairings, start with small batches to minimize waste in case the combination doesn't turn out as expected. This allows you to tweak and adjust the flavors until you find the perfect balance.

· Keep a Flavor Journal: Keep track of your flavor experiments in a journal or notebook, noting the ingredients used, the proportions, and any observations about the flavor combinations. This can help you remember successful pairings and avoid repeating unsuccessful ones in the future.

· Get Inspired by Global Cuisine: Draw inspiration from different cuisines around the world and explore traditional flavor pairings from cultures that have a rich culinary heritage. Experimenting with ingredients and flavors from different cuisines can open up a world of possibilities and inspire your own unique creations.

By understanding the principles of flavor affinities and combinations, pairing ingredients for maximum flavor impact, and experimenting with flavor pairings in your cooking, you can unlock the full potential of ingredients and create dishes that are flavorful, exciting, and memorable. So, let your creativity flow, trust your taste buds, and have fun exploring the art of flavor pairing in your culinary adventures.

# CHAPTER 18: BRINGING FLAVORFUL TRADITIONS TO YOUR KITCHEN

Bringing flavorful traditions into your kitchen is a wonderful way to connect with your heritage, honor your family's culinary legacy, and create memorable meals that celebrate culture and tradition. In this chapter, we'll explore flavorful recipes passed down through generations, delve into cultural traditions and their impact on flavor, and provide tips for incorporating family recipes into your cooking repertoire to keep tradition alive and thriving.

Flavorful Recipes Passed Down Through Generations:

Family recipes are treasures that carry memories, stories, and traditions from one generation to the next. Whether it's Grandma's secret spaghetti sauce or Aunt Maria's famous apple pie, these recipes hold a special place in our hearts and kitchens. Here are some flavorful recipes passed down through generations:

- Grandma's Chicken Soup: A comforting and nourishing soup made with homemade chicken broth, tender chicken, carrots, celery, onions, and aromatic herbs. This timeless recipe is a symbol of love and comfort and has been passed down through generations, bringing warmth and healing to countless family gatherings.
- Mom's Meatballs and Marinara: A classic Italian dish featuring tender meatballs made with a blend of ground meats, breadcrumbs, Parmesan cheese, and Italian herbs, simmered in a rich and flavorful marinara sauce. This beloved recipe is a family favorite and a staple at holiday dinners and Sunday suppers.
- Great-Grandma's Apple Strudel: A flaky and delicious pastry filled with sweet-tart apples, raisins, cinnamon, and nuts, wrapped in layers of delicate phyllo dough and baked to golden perfection. This cherished recipe has been passed down through generations and is a beloved dessert for special occasions and family gatherings.

Exploring Cultural Traditions and Their Impact on Flavor:

Cultural traditions play a significant role in shaping our culinary identities and influencing the flavors and ingredients we use in our cooking. Each culture has its own unique culinary heritage, techniques, and flavor profiles that reflect its history, geography, and values. Here are some examples of cultural traditions and their impact on flavor:

- Italian Cuisine: Known for its bold flavors, vibrant colors, and emphasis on fresh, seasonal ingredients, Italian cuisine celebrates the simplicity and abundance of nature. Ingredients like olive oil, tomatoes, garlic, basil, and Parmesan cheese are staples in Italian cooking and contribute to the rich and diverse flavor palette of the cuisine.
- Mexican Cuisine: Characterized by its bold spices, complex sauces, and vibrant colors, Mexican cuisine is a celebration of flavor and tradition. Ingredients like chili peppers, cilantro, lime, avocado, and corn are central to Mexican cooking and contribute to the bold and distinctive flavors of dishes like tacos, enchiladas, and mole sauce.
- Indian Cuisine: Known for its aromatic spices, bold flavors, and rich sauces, Indian cuisine is a feast for the senses. Ingredients like cumin, coriander, turmeric, ginger, garlic, and garam masala are essential to Indian cooking and contribute to the diverse and complex flavor profiles of dishes like curry, biryani, and samosas.

Tips for Incorporating Family Recipes into Your Cooking Repertoire:

Incorporating family recipes into your cooking repertoire is a wonderful way to preserve tradition, honor your heritage, and create meaningful connections with loved ones. Here are some tips for bringing family recipes to life in your kitchen:

- Document Family Recipes: Take the time to document family recipes by writing them down or recording them in a digital format. Include detailed instructions, measurements, and any special tips or techniques passed down from previous generations to ensure that the recipes are preserved for future generations.

· Experiment and Adapt: Don't be afraid to experiment with family recipes and adapt them to suit your taste preferences and dietary needs. Feel free to add your own twist to the recipes or substitute ingredients to make them healthier or more accessible.

· Share the Love: Share family recipes with friends and loved ones by hosting a cooking night or potluck where everyone brings a dish made from a family recipe. This is a wonderful way to celebrate tradition, foster connections, and create new memories together.

By embracing family recipes, exploring cultural traditions, and incorporating the flavors and techniques of your heritage into your cooking, you can create meaningful connections with loved ones, preserve tradition, and celebrate the rich tapestry of culinary heritage that has been passed down through generations. So, gather your loved ones, roll up your sleeves, and let the flavors of tradition inspire your culinary adventures in the kitchen.

# CHAPTER 19: THE FUTURE OF FLAVORFUL COOKING

As culinary trends evolve and palates change, the future of flavorful cooking is filled with exciting possibilities. In this chapter, we'll explore trends and innovations in flavorful cuisine, delve into the exploration of new ingredients and flavor profiles, and provide tips for staying ahead in the world of flavorful cooking to ensure your culinary creations continue to delight and inspire.

Trends and Innovations in Flavorful Cuisine:

Flavorful cuisine is constantly evolving, driven by changing tastes, cultural influences, and advancements in culinary technology. Here are some trends and innovations shaping the future of flavorful cooking:

- Plant-Based Revolution: The rise of plant-based eating is revolutionizing the culinary world, with more people embracing vegetarian, vegan, and flexitarian diets. Chefs and home cooks alike are experimenting with innovative plant-based ingredients and techniques to create flavorful dishes that rival their meat-based counterparts.

- Global Fusion: As our world becomes increasingly interconnected, chefs are drawing inspiration from diverse culinary traditions and fusing flavors and ingredients from different cultures to create exciting and innovative dishes. Global fusion cuisine celebrates the rich tapestry of flavors from around the world and encourages creativity and experimentation in the kitchen.
- Functional Foods: There is growing interest in the health benefits of certain foods and ingredients, leading to the rise of functional foods that not only taste delicious but also support health and wellbeing. From adaptogenic herbs and superfoods to gut-friendly ingredients and immune-boosting spices, functional foods are becoming an integral part of flavorful cooking.

Exploring New Ingredients and Flavor Profiles:

The exploration of new ingredients and flavor profiles is essential for pushing the boundaries of culinary creativity and innovation. Here are some emerging ingredients and flavor profiles to watch out for:

- Alternative Proteins: With the growing demand for plant-based alternatives to meat, chefs and food scientists are exploring innovative sources of protein such as jackfruit, tempeh, seitan, and lab-grown meat substitutes. These alternative proteins offer unique flavor profiles and textures that can inspire creative and flavorful dishes.

- Global Flavors: As consumers become more adventurous in their culinary tastes, there is increasing interest in exploring the diverse flavors of global cuisines. Ingredients like harissa, gochujang, za'atar, and sumac are gaining popularity for their bold and distinctive flavor profiles that add depth and complexity to dishes.
- Fermented Foods: Fermented foods like kimchi, sauerkraut, miso, and kombucha are prized for their tangy, umami-rich flavors and gut-friendly benefits. Chefs are incorporating fermented ingredients into their dishes to add depth of flavor and promote digestive health, creating a new wave of flavorful and nutritious cuisine.

Tips for Staying Ahead in the World of Flavorful Cooking:

Staying ahead in the world of flavorful cooking requires curiosity, creativity, and a willingness to experiment. Here are some tips for staying ahead and continuing to innovate in your culinary endeavors:

- Stay Curious: Keep an open mind and stay curious about new ingredients, techniques, and flavor combinations. Explore farmers markets, ethnic grocery stores, and online resources to discover unique ingredients and culinary trends that inspire your creativity.
- Experiment Freely: Don't be afraid to experiment with new ingredients and flavor profiles in your cooking. Embrace trial and error as part of the creative process and be willing to take risks and try new things. You never know what delicious discoveries you might stumble upon!
- Continuously Learn and Grow: Stay informed about the latest trends and innovations in the culinary world

by reading books, attending cooking classes and work-shops, and following chefs and food experts on social media. Continuous learning and growth are essential for staying ahead and maintaining your edge in the competitive world of flavorful cooking.

By embracing culinary trends and innovations, exploring new ingredients and flavor profiles, and staying curious and open-minded in your approach to cooking, you can ensure that your culinary creations continue to excite and inspire. So, let your imagination run wild, experiment fearlessly, and pave the way for the future of flavorful cooking.

# CHAPTER 20: CONCLUSION: EMBRACING FLAVOR IN YOUR COOKING JOURNEY

As we come to the end of this flavorful cooking adventure, it's time to reflect on the experiences we've shared, the flavors we've discovered, and the memories we've created in the kitchen. In this final chapter, we'll reflect on your flavorful cooking journey, provide tips for continuing to explore and experiment with flavor, and encourage you to embrace the joy of cooking with flavor as you continue on your culinary path.

Reflecting on Your Flavorful Cooking Adventure:

Take a moment to reflect on the journey you've embarked on throughout this book. From exploring the basics of flavor building to mastering the art of flavor pairing, you've learned valuable skills and techniques that have transformed your cooking. Think about the delicious recipes you've tried, the new ingredients you've discovered, and the flavors that have delighted your taste buds along the way.

Consider how your cooking has evolved and grown throughout this journey. Have you become more adventurous in your flavor choices? Have you discovered new favorite ingredients or flavor combinations? Take pride in how far you've come and the delicious meals you've created along the way.

Tips for Continuing to Explore and Experiment with Flavor:

Your flavorful cooking journey doesn't have to end here—it's just the beginning of a lifelong adventure in the kitchen. Here are some tips for continuing to explore and experiment with flavor:

- Keep Learning: The world of flavor is vast and ever-changing, so don't stop learning and expanding your culinary knowledge. Experiment with new ingredients, techniques, and cuisines to keep your cooking fresh and exciting.
- Be Fearless: Don't be afraid to push the boundaries of your culinary creativity and try new things. Embrace experimentation and be willing to take risks in the kitchen —you never know what delicious discoveries you might make!
- Trust Your Taste Buds: Your taste buds are your greatest asset in the kitchen, so trust them to guide you as you cook. Pay attention to the flavors, textures, and aromas of your dishes, and don't be afraid to adjust seasoning or ingredients to achieve the perfect balance of flavor.

Embracing the Joy of Cooking with Flavor:

Above all else, remember to embrace the joy of cooking with flavor. Cooking is not just about nourishing your body—it's about feeding your soul, expressing your creativity, and connecting with others. Whether you're cooking for yourself, your family, or your friends, let the joy of flavor infuse every moment in the kitchen.

Celebrate the simple pleasures of chopping fresh herbs, sizzling onions in a hot pan, and savoring the aroma of a dish as it simmers on the stove. Cherish the laughter shared around the dining table, the stories exchanged over a delicious meal, and the memories created with each bite.

As you continue on your flavorful cooking journey, remember that the most important ingredient is love. Infuse your cooking with passion, creativity, and joy, and let the flavors you create nourish not only your body but also your spirit.

So, go forth with confidence, curiosity, and an open heart, and let the flavors of the world inspire your culinary adventures. Embrace the joy of cooking with flavor, and may your kitchen always be filled with love, laughter, and deliciousness. Happy cooking!

proceed to Appendix: Flavorful Recipe Index · Index of All Recipes Featured in the Book, Categorized by Course and Flavor Profile

ChatGPT

Appendix: Flavorful Recipe Index

Welcome to the Flavorful Recipe Index, where you'll find a comprehensive list of all the delicious recipes featured in this book, categorized by course and flavor profile. Whether you're looking for mouthwatering appetizers, hearty main courses, or indulgent desserts, this index will guide you to the perfect recipe to satisfy your cravings and ignite your culinary creativity.

**Appetizers:**

1. Bruschetta with Tomato, Basil, and Balsamic Glaze
2. Spicy Hummus with Fresh Vegetables
3. Caprese Skewers with Balsamic Glaze
4. Spinach and Artichoke Dip
5. Mango Salsa with Homemade Tortilla Chips

**Soups and Salads:**

1. Roasted Butternut Squash Soup with Sage and Crispy Bacon
2. Greek Salad with Feta and Kalamata Olives
3. Thai Coconut Curry Soup with Shrimp
4. Quinoa Salad with Roasted Vegetables
5. Caesar Salad with Homemade Croutons

**Main Courses:**

1. Lemon Garlic Roast Chicken with Rosemary Potatoes
2. Spaghetti Carbonara with Pancetta and Peas
3. Grilled Salmon with Honey Dijon Glaze
4. Vegetable Stir-Fry with Tofu and Ginger Soy Sauce
5. Beef and Broccoli Stir-Fry with Jasmine Rice

## Sides and Accompaniments:

1. Garlic Parmesan Roasted Brussels Sprouts
2. Lemon Herb Rice Pilaf
3. Creamy Mashed Potatoes with Chives
4. Sauteed Green Beans with Almonds
5. Quinoa Pilaf with Mushrooms and Thyme

## Desserts:

1. Classic Chocolate Chip Cookies
2. Vanilla Bean Panna Cotta with Fresh Berries
3. Apple Crisp with Cinnamon Oat Topping
4. Chocolate Lava Cakes with Raspberry Coulis
5. Tiramisu with Espresso and Mascarpone

## Drinks and Beverages:

1. Classic Margarita with Fresh Lime Juice
2. Strawberry Basil Lemonade
3. Mojito with Mint and Lime
4. Iced Matcha Latte with Almond Milk
5. Spiced Hot Chocolate with Whipped Cream

## Special Dietary Needs:

1. Gluten-Free Quinoa Salad with Roasted Vegetables
2. Dairy-Free Thai Coconut Curry Soup with Shrimp
3. Paleo Lemon Garlic Roast Chicken with Rosemary Potatoes
4. Vegan Vegetable Stir-Fry with Tofu and Ginger Soy Sauce
5. Keto Beef and Broccoli Stir-Fry with Cauliflower Rice

This index serves as a handy reference guide for all the flavorful recipes you'll find in this book. Whether you're planning a weeknight dinner, a weekend brunch, or a special occasion celebration, you'll find a wide range of delicious recipes to inspire your culinary adventures. Happy cooking and bon appétit!

proceed to Glossary of Flavor Terms · Definitions of Key Terms and Concepts Related to Flavor in Cooking

ChatGPT

Glossary of Flavor Terms

As you embark on your flavorful cooking journey, it's helpful to familiarize yourself with key terms and concepts related to flavor. This glossary provides definitions to enhance your understanding of flavor and its role in cooking:

1. Umami: Often referred to as the "fifth taste," umami is a savory flavor that is characteristic of foods rich in glutamate, such as meats, aged cheeses, tomatoes, and soy sauce.

2. Aromatics: Aromatics are ingredients that add fragrance and flavor to dishes, typically through their essential oils. Common aromatics include onions, garlic, ginger, and herbs like rosemary and thyme.

3. Maillard Reaction: The Maillard reaction is a chemical reaction that occurs when proteins and sugars in food are exposed to heat, resulting in browning and the development of complex, savory flavors. This reaction is responsible for the delicious flavors of grilled meats, toasted bread, and roasted vegetables.

4. Mise en Place: Mise en place is a French culinary term that means "putting in place." It refers to the practice of prepping and organizing all ingredients and equipment before starting to cook, ensuring a smooth and efficient cooking process.

5. Deglazing: Deglazing is a cooking technique that involves adding liquid (such as wine, broth, or vinegar) to a pan to loosen and dissolve the flavorful browned bits that form on the bottom during cooking. This technique helps to create rich sauces and adds depth of flavor to dishes.

6. Reduction: Reduction is the process of simmering a liquid (such as stock, wine, or sauce) over heat to evaporate water and concentrate flavors, resulting in a thicker consistency and intensified flavor.

7. Infusion: Infusion is the process of steeping ingredients (such as herbs, spices, or aromatics) in a liquid (such as water, oil, or alcohol) to extract their flavors. Infusions are commonly used to flavor sauces, soups, and beverages.

8. Marination: Marination is the process of soaking food (such as meat, poultry, or vegetables) in a flavorful liquid (such as a marinade or brine) to impart flavor, tenderize, and enhance moisture retention before cooking.

9. Seasoning: Seasoning refers to the addition of salt, herbs, spices, and other flavorings to enhance the taste of food. Proper seasoning is essential for balancing flavors and bringing out the natural tastes of ingredients.

10. Tasting Notes: Tasting notes are descriptions of the flavors, aromas, and textures perceived when sampling food or beverages. They often include descriptors such as sweet, salty, sour, bitter, umami, fruity, floral, spicy, creamy, and nutty.

By familiarizing yourself with these flavor terms and concepts, you'll gain a deeper appreciation for the role of flavor in cooking and develop the skills to create delicious and memorable dishes. So, embrace the language of flavor, experiment with different ingredients and techniques, and let your taste buds guide you on your flavorful cooking journey.

proceed to Acknowledgments · Recognizing Those Who Contributed to the Creation of Cooking with Flavor

ChatGPT

Acknowledgments

Creating "Cooking with Flavor: Delicious Recipes for Every Palate" has been a labor of love, and I am deeply grateful to all those who have contributed to its creation. Their support, encouragement, and expertise have been invaluable in bringing this book to life.

First and foremost, I would like to express my gratitude to the countless chefs, home cooks, and food enthusiasts whose passion for flavor has inspired the recipes and ideas shared in this book. Your dedication to the culinary arts is truly commendable, and it is a privilege to be part of such a vibrant and creative community.

I would also like to extend my heartfelt thanks to the team at the publishing house who believed in this project from the beginning and worked tirelessly to bring it to fruition. Your dedication, professionalism, and enthusiasm have been instrumental in shaping this book into what it is today.

Special thanks to my family and friends for their unwavering support and encouragement throughout the writing process. Your love, encouragement, and willingness to taste-test countless recipes have been a constant source of inspiration and motivation.

Last but not least, I would like to express my deepest appreciation to the readers of this book. It is my sincere hope that the recipes, tips, and ideas shared within these pages will bring joy, flavor, and inspiration to your culinary adventures. Thank you for allowing me to be part of your cooking journey.

With gratitude,

[Your Name]

proceed to About the Author · Biography of the Author (Jim Stephens) and Their Culinary Journey

ChatGPT

About the Author

Jim Stephens is a passionate food enthusiast, cookbook author, and culinary explorer with a deep love for flavor-filled cooking. Born and raised in a family where food was central to gatherings and celebrations, Jim's culinary journey began at an early age, watching his grandmother and mother create delicious meals from scratch using fresh, seasonal ingredients.

Inspired by the sights, sounds, and aromas of the kitchen, Jim developed a keen interest in cooking and began experimenting with recipes and flavors in his own kitchen. Over the years, he honed his skills through self-study, cooking classes, and hands-on experience, exploring a wide range of cuisines and culinary techniques along the way.

Driven by a desire to share his passion for flavor-filled cooking with others, Jim embarked on a writing journey to create "Cooking with Flavor: Delicious Recipes for Every Palate." Drawing on his experiences as a home cook, food blogger, and recipe developer, Jim crafted a collection of mouthwatering recipes, helpful tips, and culinary insights to inspire readers to embrace the joy of cooking with flavor.

When he's not in the kitchen experimenting with new recipes or exploring farmers markets for fresh ingredients, Jim can be found sharing his love for food and cooking on his blog and social media channels. He believes that food has the power to bring people together, create lasting memories, and nourish the body and soul—a philosophy that shines through in his approach to cooking and writing.

Jim resides in [Location], where he continues to pursue his passion for flavorful cooking, discovering new ingredients, and sharing his culinary adventures with others. He hopes that "Cooking with Flavor" will inspire readers to unleash their creativity in the kitchen, experiment with new flavors and ingredients, and savor the joys of home-cooked meals shared with loved ones.

Write a book blurb for all the above text. Cooking with Flavor: Delicious Recipes for Every Palate

ChatGPT

Introducing "Cooking with Flavor: Delicious Recipes for Every Palate" by Jim Stephens—an exquisite culinary journey packed with mouthwatering recipes, invaluable cooking insights, and a celebration of the art of flavor. From the basics of flavor building to the exploration of global cuisine, this book is a treasure trove of inspiration for home cooks of all skill levels.

Embark on a flavorful adventure as you explore the importance of flavor in cooking, learn about key ingredients and techniques, and discover how to enhance the taste of your dishes. With chapters dedicated to everything from appetizers and main courses to desserts and beverages, you'll find a wealth of delicious recipes to suit every taste and occasion.

Delight in the vibrant flavors of hearty soups, vibrant salads, succulent meat dishes, and creative vegetarian creations. Elevate your cooking with tips for incorporating seasonal and local ingredients, experimenting with flavor pairings, and embracing the joy of cooking with love and passion.

Written with warmth, expertise, and a deep love for food, "Cooking with Flavor" is more than just a cookbook—it's a culinary companion that will inspire you to unleash your creativity in the kitchen and create unforgettable meals that nourish the body and soul. Whether you're a seasoned chef or a novice cook, this book is sure to become a beloved resource in your kitchen. So, grab your apron, sharpen your knives, and get ready to embark on a flavorful journey like no other.

list 20 keywords for all the above text.
ChatGPT

1. Cooking
2. Flavor
3. Recipes
4. Culinary
5. Inspiration
6. Ingredients
7. Techniques
8. Exploration
9. Global cuisine

10. Home cooking
11. Creativity
12. Passion
13. Taste
14. Seasonal
15. Local
16. Experimentation
17. Joy
18. Nourishment
19. Skills
20. Celebration

List 3 Bisac categories for this book
ChatGPT

1. COOKING / General
2. COOKING / Courses & Dishes / General
3. COOKING / Methods / General

write three 200 word positive book reviews.

ChatGPT

Review 1: "Cooking with Flavor: Delicious Recipes for Every Palate" by Jim Stephens is an absolute gem for anyone looking to elevate their culinary skills and infuse their dishes with mouthwatering flavor. Stephens' passion for cooking shines through in every recipe, and his thorough explanations of flavor profiles, techniques, and ingredient pairings make this book a valuable resource for home cooks of all levels. From savory appetizers to decadent desserts, each recipe is thoughtfully crafted to tantalize the taste buds and inspire creativity in the kitchen. What sets this book apart is Stephens' emphasis on using fresh, seasonal ingredients and his innovative approach to flavor combinations. Whether you're a novice cook or a seasoned chef, you'll find plenty of inspiration and practical tips to enhance your cooking skills and impress your family and friends. "Cooking with Flavor" is more than just a cookbook—it's a culinary adventure that will leave you feeling inspired, confident, and hungry for more delicious meals.

Review 2: "Jim Stephens has truly outdone himself with 'Cooking with Flavor: Delicious Recipes for Every Palate.' This cookbook is a treasure trove of culinary delights, offering a diverse array of recipes that are sure to satisfy even the most discerning palate. Stephens' writing style is engaging and accessible, making it easy for readers to follow along and replicate his mouthwatering creations in their own kitchens. What I love most about this book is Stephens' emphasis on flavor—each recipe is bursting with vibrant, bold flavors that elevate every dish to new heights. Whether you're craving comforting soups, refreshing salads, or indulgent desserts, you'll find something to love in this cookbook. With clear instructions, helpful tips, and stunning photography, 'Cooking with Flavor' is a must-have addition to any cook's library. Trust me, once you start cooking from this book, you won't be able to put it down!"

Review 3: "I can't say enough good things about 'Cooking with Flavor' by Jim Stephens. This cookbook has quickly become my go-to resource for delicious, flavorful recipes that never fail to impress. Stephens' passion for food and cooking is evident on every page, and his recipes are as accessible as they are inspiring. What I appreciate most about this book is Stephens' emphasis on using fresh, wholesome ingredients and his creative approach to flavor pairing. Whether you're a seasoned cook or just starting out in the kitchen, you'll find plenty of recipes to suit your skill level and taste preferences. From elegant appetizers to hearty main courses to irresistible desserts, there's something for everyone in this cookbook. Plus, Stephens' friendly writing style and helpful tips make it feel like you're cooking alongside a trusted friend. If you're looking to take your cooking to the next level and infuse your dishes with delicious flavor, do yourself a favor and pick up a copy of 'Cooking with Flavor' today. You won't be disappointed!"

Milton Keynes UK
Ingram Content Group UK Ltd.
UKHW040329031224
452051UK00011B/311

9 798330 600502